MY HERB GARDEN

Written By: Anna DiGilio

All rights reserved. No part of this publication may be reproduced, distributed, or transmitted in any form or by any means, including photocopying, recording, or other electronic or mechanical methods, without the prior written permission of the publisher, except in the case of brief quotations embodied in critical reviews and certain other noncommercial uses permitted by copyright law.

For permission requests, write to the publisher:
Laprea Publishing
info@lapreapublishing.com

Website: www.GuidedReaders.com

ISBN: 978-1-64579-593-3

© 2019 Anna DiGilio

Photo Credits:
Cover, Title Page: Depositphotos; Oksixx. 3: Depositphotos; Elena Schweitzer. 4: Depositphotos; Mavoimages. 5 (top): Depositphotos; LiliGraphie. 5 (bottom): Depositphotos; Dlexraths. 6 (top/front): Depositphotos; Alexynder. 6 (top/back): Depositphotos; Strelok. 6 (bottom): Depositphotos; VadimVasenin. 7 (top): Depositphotos; Lovelymama. 7 (bottom): Depositphotos; Anna_Shepulova. 8 (top): Depositphotos; Fisfra. 8 (bottom): Depositphotos; Robynmac. 9 (top): Depositphotos; Anskuw. 9 (bottom): Depositphotos; Chiociolla. 10 (top): Depositphotos; Svetas. 10 (bottom): Depositphotos; Anna_Shepulova. 11 (top): Depositphotos; Bit245. 11 (bottom): Depositphotos; VadimVasenin. 12 (top): Depositphotos; StephanieFrey. 12 (bottom): Depositphotos; Simply.

TABLE OF CONTENTS

What Are Herbs? .... Page 5

Types of Herbs .... Page 7

Growing Herbs .... Page 12

Glossary .... Page 13

This is my garden. It is full of <u>herbs</u>.

What Are Herbs?

Herbs are plants you can eat. They are not fruits.

They are not veggies. They still taste good.

Types of Herbs

This is basil. I put it on pasta.

This is thyme. I put it on chicken.

This is mint. I like it on ice cream.

This is rosemary. I bake it in bread!

Herbs make food yummy. They make cooking fun!

These are basil plants being planted.

Growing Herbs

Herbs are easy to grow. You should try it.

These are rosemary plants being trimmed.

GLOSSARY

<u>herbs</u>
any plants with leaves, seeds, or flowers used for flavoring food, medicine, or perfume